CARING FOR YOUR RABBIT

HOW TO CARE FOR YOUR RABBIT
AND EVERYTHING YOU NEED TO
KNOW TO KEEP THEM WELL

BY

DR. GORDON ROBERTS BVSC MRCVS

TABLE OF CONTENTS

Introduction
Rabbit Breeds
Characteristics
Choosing the Right Rabbit For You
Behaviour
Housing
Introducing your rabbit to your existing pets
Daily Routine Health & Hygiene
First Aid
Reproduction
Neutering (also known as 'altering')
Ailments
Natural Remedies
Poisonous Plants
Top Ten Tips for a healthy, happy rabbit
Frequently Asked Questions Useful Addresses

INTRODUCTION

Wild rabbits cover the entire world, from the Tropics to the Arctic, and have adjusted to living in various climates and habitats whether it be wild tundra, snow covered mountains or deserts and forests.

Believe it or not, most species of wild rabbit are solitary beings, the exception is the European Rabbit (originally found in Western Europe - Southern France, Portugal and Spain); they are social creatures and live in colonies which we know as warrens. The tunnels and dens can cover a massive area with several entry and exit points, and are run by dominate males who have several females who also form their own hierachy.

This same hierachy is reflected in many other mammal species. Their warning signal for impending danger is the thumping of their hind leg - remember Thumper the rabbit in the Walt Disney Film?

The domesticated rabbit originates from the European Rabbit and is now common around the world. Over 2000 years ago, ancient trading people travelling the seas realised rabbit meat was a good source of food and their fur had a trading value. Because of their journeys of exploration around the world, their rabbits were introduced to other countries and so the domestic rabbits' history begins.

Domestication meant that the rabbit was protected from their natural predators, and the need for camouflage was no longer important and, with selective breeding from around 1700 we started to see a variety of new fur colours introduced (see section on Common Breeds). Around this time domesticated rabbits also became

heavier – they no longer needed to flee from danger. By the late 1800s, rabbits were being bred to create different sizes and types of fur, as well as for different colours.

RABBIT BREEDS

There are many different pet rabbit breeds in a wide range of shapes, sizes and colours, but they are all part of the European Rabbit (Oryctolagus Cuniculus) species. Believe it or not, there are well over 50 pet rabbit breeds and we have listed the most popular ones below, all of which make great indoor or outdoor pets.

Lop Rabbits

You can easily recognize the lop rabbit by its long floppy ears. The ears of the English Lop are fairly large at up to 50cm. The ears of lop eared rabbits have lost all movement, and even their skull has been altered by the weight of them, and this in turn has adversely affected their hearing.

There are also smaller breeds of lop rabbit, the Dwarf Lop and the Mini Lop. The smaller variety are cute, gentle and make a very friendly pet rabbit, and come in a variety of colours.

Mini Lop Rabbit

Weight: Females & Males : 6.5lbs
Physical Attributes: Compact, muscular, many colours.
Personality: The mini lop is a very nice breed, sometimes a little less lively than other breeds, but do love attention.
Coat Type and Grooming: If you have an adult rabbit, the only time you should groom them is when they are molting – a mini lop can die from eating too much of its hair. If you have a baby lop they lose their baby fur gradually.

Holland Lop Rabbit

Varieties: Agouti, White, Shaded, Dark color with silver or gold tipped hairs spread throughout the coat; Wide Band.
Weight: Females & Males: 4lbs
Physical Attributes: The Holland Lop has a short body but bulky, and seems to be a large rabbit in a small body with a short thick, large head. The ears are short and lopped.
Personality: On the whole they are fairly calm, but the females can be shy and skittish.
Coat Type and Grooming: A medium-length coat that sometimes requires a bit of extra grooming when molting.

Dutch Rabbits

This rabbit is a 19th century breed, and is probably the most recognizable – they have the saddle markings, i.e. the front of the rabbit's head, the front section of their body and part of their hind feet are white, with the sides of the head, ears and rear half of their body coloured.

Varieties: White and black, white and blue are the most common, tortoiseshell, chocolate, yellow, but there will only be two combinations of colour on each rabbit.
Weight: Females & Males : 5lb (2.2kg)
Physical Attributes: Small, bi-coloured.
Personality: friendly rabbits, a good first rabbit to have as a pet.
Coat Type and Grooming: A medium-length coat that sometimes requires a bit of extra grooming when molting.

English Rabbits (also known as English Spot Rabbits)

This rabbit is also a 19th century breed, like the Dutch above. The English has usual colouring which makes it instantly recognizable. The coat is patterned with a narrow band of colour down the spine, dark ears, dark eye circles and markings on the flanks with a butterfly marking on the nose.

Varieties: Blue, black, tortoiseshell, chocolate or grey on white.
Weight: Females & Males : 8 lb (3.6kg).
Physical Attributes: Medium size, patterned.
Personality: Gentle and friendly, but very active.
Coat Type and Grooming: A medium-length coat that sometimes requires a bit of extra grooming when molting.

Angora Rabbits

Angora rabbits are one of the oldest and most popular breeds of rabbit, and are the only rabbits bred for their fur. Their coat (or wool) is very long and soft and can reach up to 12cm in length and will require a lot more care than other rabbit breeds. You will have to be prepared to brush, clean and trim regularly.

Varieties: Blue, Gold.
Weight: Females & Males : 5-6 lb (2.5kg-4kg).
Physical Attributes: Medium, patterned.
Personality: Charming, Gentle and friendly, but very active.
Coat Type and Grooming: Long soft fur, requires brushing every day and regular stripping.

Rex Rabbit

This breed was first seen in France in the 1920s and is easily recognized by its short, upright, thick fur. Because the guard hairs are the same length as the underhair, the coat looks and feels like velvet. The Rex has been crossed with many other breeds, so we are now seeing Chinchilla Rex, Rex Dalmation, Rex Tortoiseshell and so on.

Varieties:. Black, Blue, Black Otter, Broken (Includes Tricolor), Californian, Castor, Chinchilla, Chocolate, Lilac, Lynx, Opal, Red, Sable, Seal, White
Weight: Males: 7-9.5lbs; Females: 8-10lbs
Physical Attributes: Large breed with upright ears. Fur feels live velvet.
Personality: Friendly, not particularly active, quite happy to play and sit on your lap.
Coat Type and Grooming: Short and very plush, thick and feels like velvet. No need to groom, simply moisten hands with water and run over the rabbits coat backwards to remove loose hair and static.

Hotot

The Hotot originally comes from the Normandy region in France (Blanc de Hotot) and takes its name from that area. The rabbit is a medium sized breed and the colouring is always white with black eye bands, there are no variations to this colouring.

Varieties: White with black eye bands.
Weight: Males & Females: 9lbs
Physical Attributes: Breed is white except for a thin band of colour around each eye.
Personality: Quite calm and enjoy attention. They like toys are curious and like to be mentally stimulated.
Coat Type and Grooming: Short coat, weekly grooming when shedding may be necessary.

Dwarf Hotot

The Dwarf Hotot was bred down from the standard Hotot in the 1970s. The dwarf hotot is also only ever white and appears to be wearing eyeliner, with its black eye bands.

Varieties: White with coloured markings
Weight: Males: 2.5lbs ; Females: 2.5lbs
Physical Attributes: Very short, round body. Ears are upright, short and thick. Breed is white except for a thin band of colour around each eye.
Personality: Quite calm and enjoy attention. They like toys are curious and like to be mentally stimulated.
Coat Type and Grooming:
Short coat, weekly grooming when shedding may be necessary.

Flemish Giant Rabbit

Originated in Belgium, this breed of rabbit is what it says on the box – a giant of a rabbit, weighing in at over 14lbs, the largest breed of rabbit. Not recommended for the first time rabbit owner and definitely not for children as they are so heavy. In general the larger the rabbit the more laid back and relaxed they are.

Varieties: Steel grey, light grey, black, blue, white, sandy, fawn.
Weight: Males & Females 11-14lb
Physical Attributes: Massive, shoulders and body long and powerful in appearance, very solid, long ears and large head.
Personality: Quite calm and enjoy attention. "The gentle giant breeds".
Coat Type and Grooming:
Short coat, weekly grooming when shedding may be necessary.

Common breeds:

- American Fuzzy Lop
- Holland Lop
- Florida White
- Mini Rex
- English Spot
- Chinchilla
- Checkered Giant
- French Angora
- Giant Angora
- Brittania Petite
- Mini Lop
- Havana
- Belgian Hare
- Harlequin
- American Sable
- Cinnamon
- Hotot
- Giant Chinchilla
- Dwarf Hotot
- Dutch
- Himalayan
- English Angora
- Satin Angora
- Californian
- Creme D'Argent
- Rex Flemish Giant

Less Common Breeds:

- American Lop - French Satin
- Beveren Lop - Velveteen Satin - Mini
- Giant Lop - Mini Plush Silver
- Himalayan Netherland Dwarf Silver
- Fox
- Jersey Wooly New Zealand Silver
- Marten
- Lionhead Palomino Tan
- Lilac Polish
- Lop - English Rhinelander

CHARACTERISTICS

Below is a table showing the most common breeds and their characteristics – hopefully this will give you an easy-to-use-guide to choosing the perfect bunny for you and your lifestyle.

Breed	Size Large >10lb	Size Medium 6-10lb	Size Small 2-6lb	Colours	Fur Short	Fur Long	Ear type Lop	Ear type Medium	Ear type Short	Temperament Calm	Temperament Excitable
American		✓		Blue/white	✓			✓		✓	
Angora		✓		6 colours		✓		✓		✓	
Chinchilla		✓			✓			✓		✓	
Dutch			✓	6 colours	✓			✓		✓	
Dwarf Hotot			✓	White dark eyes	✓				✓		✓
English Spot		✓		7 colours dark spots	✓			✓		✓	
Flemish Giant	✓				✓			✓		✓	✓
Harlequin		✓		4 colours	✓			✓		✓	
Rex		✓		Multi	✓			✓		✓	
Himalayan Rex			✓	White w/ black tips	✓			✓		✓	✓
Mini Rex			✓	Multi	✓			✓			✓
Satin		✓		Multi	✓			✓		✓	
Mini Satin			✓	Red, white	✓			✓			✓
Polish			✓	5 colours	✓			✓			✓
Lop		✓		many	✓		✓			✓	
Tan			✓	Black tan	✓			✓		✓	

Tip : Rex rabbits lack the heavy protective fur on their pads, so you must house them on surfaces that provide some softness.

CHOOSING THE RIGHT RABBIT FOR YOU

Rabbits are considered to be interactive pets, and live between 7 and 10 years – therefore they will need a fair amount of your time to play with them and keep them entertained! Rabbits need care and affection to put them at ease and make

them feel safe and secure and happy. If a rabbit is neglected it can become timid and be nippy, it will then be considered vicious when all it is doing it is reverting to 'wild rabbit self preservation' mode.

Indoor vs Outdoor Rabbit

Deciding on whether you would like your rabbit to live indoors with you or outdoors in a hutch is naturally only a choice you can make. Both Indoor and outdoor rabbits require their own cage as a safe place and also need adequate exercise and attention. Indoor rabbits will need a litter tray and can be trained to use the tray, they also need exercise so will generally run around your house, but make sure it is rabbit-proof before you let them run around and explore, e.g. all low cupboards should all be securely closed! Indoor rabbits are also at risk of being stepped on, sat on, even inadvertently kicked.

If some sort of physical contact has occurred or you think may have, the most important thing (and this holds true for any emergency) is to contact your vet immediately. Rabbits kept outdoors will need a hutch positioned in a sheltered position and out of direct sunlight. They will also need plenty of exercise, which can be in the form of a rabbit run or if your garden is secure and there are no poisonous plants they can be free to run around, but you will need to keep an eye on them.

Multiple Rabbit Households

Rabbits need companionship, whether it be you or another rabbit or another pet. However, if you plan to have more than one rabbit, then female rabbits (does) can usually live together quite happily, but a male rabbit (buck) is best on his own. Please read the chapters on Neutering and Reproduction if you do have a buck and a doe or plan to breed from your rabbits.

BEHAVIOUR

Domesticated rabbits were bred to be docile and comfortable around people. Wild rabbits on the other hand are still wild and will panic if confined and will bite. However, if a domestic rabbit is neglected and not given enough attention, they can revert back to their wild state. Rabbits never lose their instinct as a prey animal, so if scared will make a run for cover.

Rabbits are intelligent and sociable animals, active and very inquisitive. They do require interaction with their owners on a very regular basis, otherwise they will become bored and if they don't have enough activity their health will certainly suffer. You should provide an interesting

environment for them so they can do what comes naturally – hopping, foraging and standing up on their hind legs - these are all natural activities for them, and should be encouraged. They also enjoy playing with other friendly rabbits, other pets and people.

Litter Training

The majority of mature rabbits that have been brought up in hutches will choose one place in their hutch in which to use as a toilet. Place the litter tray in their cage in the same place and they will start to use the tray. Once they use it regularly, you can then place a litter tray outside the cage, and place a few of their droppings in the litter tray to give it their scent – they should start using the litter tray from there on.

If your rabbit is a youngster and less than 3 months, you may have a few teething problems – if they haven't learned yet to use just one place in their cage to go to the toilet, getting them to learn to use a litter tray outside the cage will be problematical and a bit hit and miss – so to speak! Be patient though, keep an eye on them and get used to the signs of when they are about to urinate or defecate. If they look as if they are about to, by backing up or pushing their bottoms against a wall or raising their tail, this could mean they are about to go, so quickly put bunny back in their cage. This will help teach them that they should urinate/defecate in their cage. Once they use their cage regularly, then you can introduce the litter tray into the cage until they use that, then put a litter tray outside the cage.

HOUSING

Rabbits are not designed to live in a confined space. Hutches were originally used by the Victorians when they kept rabbits in backyards as a source of cheap meat, and were housed on a short term basis while they were fattened up. Under the Animal Welfare Act 2006, rabbit owners are required by law to meet their rabbit's welfare needs – which includes providing a suitable environment.

The Rabbit Welfare Association recommend a minimum hutch size of at least 6' x 2' which allows rabbits some room to move, stand on their hind legs, and enough space for the food, toilet and sleeping areas to be kept apart. They should be able to perform at least 3 consecutive hops. Larger breeds will need more space than this.

A hutch should not be their only living space – it should be attached to a secure run of at least 8' x 4'. Bear in mind, these are the minimum recommendations – as with most things in life, bigger is better!

Location and design

Their living area should be sheltered; out of direct sunlight with some shade, and also against driving wind or rain. It should also provide a hiding area where your rabbit can hide away and feel secure from predators.

The hutch should be raised on legs to prevent rising damp and deter vermin. The roof should be covered with roofing felt to allow rain water to drain off.

Safety

Unfortunately, each year many pet rabbits are snatched by predators. You need to make sure your rabbits are safe from foxes, dogs, cats and birds of prey. Strong mesh is better than chicken wire.

Stimulation

Rabbits are very social animals, and should be kept at least in pairs as they rely on the companionship from another rabbit

– they love to snuggle together, groom each other and keep each other warm. The best pairing is a neutered male and a neutered female. Keep them occupied with toys such as tunnels, plant pots or even a cardboard box. Scatter food around to encourage them forage rather than feeding from a bowl, and ensure they have constant access to hay.

INTRODUCING YOUR RABBIT TO YOUR EXISTING PETS

Like you, your new rabbit will be nervous when experiencing something new and unknown. Being in a household with other pets will give your rabbit companionship, but it goes without saying you should ensure your rabbit is safe at all times. Cats and dogs can make good companions, but never forget they still possess a carnivore instinct, so you should supervise when they are together, as any responsible parent would with children.

Rabbits have a territorial instinct naturally instilled in them, so if you want to introduce another rabbit you should do so on neutral territory. Find an area as large and safe as possible, both rabbits should enter this area at the same time – then simply watch their actions.

One may be more interested in the other, they may stare at each other for a while, and after a bit of running around they could simply end up doing their own thing. You have to be aware that there could be some aggression shown and a fight may break out. If this happens, split them up immediately, but don't give up, try the process again later in the day, or wait until the next day.

You can keep doing this as many times as necessary, eventually you will see them happily sitting together or even grooming each other. Even if they seem happy with each other from the first introduction, make sure you keep them separate overnight – you need to be keeping an eye on them until you are really sure they are best buddy bunnies.

DAILY ROUTINE

Nutrition

Feeding your rabbit the correct diet is vital to their health - research has shown that most of the common diseases that rabbits suffer from can be prevented by feeding them a healthy diet.

Feeding the incorrect diet can result in overgrown teeth and dental, disease obesity, sore eyes, conjunctivitis gut stasis and fly strike

What is the best diet for your rabbit?

The best diet is one that mimics as closely as possible what wild rabbits eat. They need a high fibre diet, so the bulk of your rabbit's diet should be grass and hay. Ensure that the hay is good quality meadow or timothy hay, it should be sweet smelling and not dusty. It should be stored carefully so it doesn't become damp or mouldy. Hay racks are available for rabbits to prevent the hay from being contaminated by droppings. Allow your rabbit direct access to grass to allow it to graze. Lawnmower clippings should not be fed.

It is important to provide your rabbit with fresh vegetables and greens on a daily basis - such as carrot tops, cabbage, parsley, celery leaves, basil, broccoli, kale etc. They should be washed before feeding.

What about commercial rabbit food?

Rabbits thrive on hay, grass and vegetables alone, but sometimes owners want to feed a commercial mix as well. Lots of rabbits will only eat certain components of mixed 'muesli-type' mixes (they pick out the tasty bits and leave the rest) which risks causing an unbalanced diet and nutrient deficiencies - leading to the health problems mentioned previously. A high quality 'nugget' mix, such as 'Burgess Excel' is a far better choice as all the nutrients are present in each nugget. Care should be taken not to overfeed commercial food as this will lead to obesity and other health problems.

What about treats?

Many commercial treats are high in fat and carbohydrate and should be avoided as they risk causing tummy upsets and obesity. Healthy, natural treats can be given in moderation.

How should I change my rabbit's diet?

Sudden changes in diet must be avoided. Any changes should be made gradually over the course of a couple of weeks to allow the digestive system time to adjust. Mix the new food in with their current food, at a ratio of 20:80 for 3-4 days and monitor for any signs of weight loss, diarrhoea, or bloating - if all is ok then increase to 60:40 for another 3-4 days, then 80:20, then finally to 100% of the new mix. Introduce grass and greens gradually to reduce the chance of diarrhoea.

Fresh water should always be available. Some studies have shown that rabbits drink better from bowls rather than bottles, so both should be offered. Remember to check your rabbit's water daily, especially in colder weather when it can freeze, if housed outside.

Exercise

Your rabbit needs regular opportunities to take exercise and hop about and should not be kept in the hutch or cage for long periods of time. They need to be allowed out to run around and do the things that bunnies do naturally for at least 8 hours a day.

Handling

Regular handling of your rabbit from an early age or from when you take on your rabbit will ensure they are used to you and will feel safe and content when sitting on your lap being stroked. However, you must know the correct way to pick up a rabbit.

Injuries to rabbit's backs are common and are generally due to not being picked up correctly. Your rabbit's rear needs to be supported by one hand with your other hand under their chest. Never pick your rabbit up by its ears.

Grooming

Grooming is not strictly necessary for a rabbit, unless you have one of the long-haired breeds - Angora. However, it does give you the opportunity to check your rabbit's condition, feeling any lumps or bumps and the rabbit will also become accustomed to being handled.

Simple health checks

To ensure a healthy, happy bunny you should carry out these basic health checks regularly:

Teeth – eating well, no dribbling;

Tearducts – no runny ears or cloudy discharge;

Clean bottom – no urine staining and especially no faeces;

Parasites – fleas, mites (walking dandruff), flies (flystrike);

Nails – not too long;

Ears – clean, odour free.

DAILY ROUTINE

So long as you are feeding your rabbit with the correct food, they have fresh water and you keep their hutches clean, give them plenty of exercise and cuddles you can't go far wrong. However, health checks are important and, if not carried out regularly, can lead to far more serious conditions, even life-threatening ones. More detailed information on some of the items listed below can be found in our Ailments section.

Nutrition – it is important to feed your rabbit the correct food and in the right quantities;

Vaccination – very important to protect against Myxomatosis and VHD;

Parasites – check their fur and skin for signs of dandruff

Diarrhea – this is very serious for rabbits, contact your vet

Constipation – if your rabbit has not passed faecal pellets for 8hrs or more, this is an emergency, contact your vet.

Teeth – their teeth grow continually and a lack of a good quality, high fibre diet prevents the teeth from wearing down appropriately, causing serious health problems

Tearducts – these can become blocked, check for discharge; Bottom – check your rabbits button to ensure that it is clean with no faeces stuck to the fur, otherwise this could lead to Flystrike (

Nails – if your rabbit isn't exercising on hard ground, then you may need to have their nails clipped;

Ears – mites, infections and accumulation of wax should be treated immediately as not doing so can quickly become an emergency.

Zoonotic diseases – diseases that can be transferred from animals to humans, can include salmonella and ringworm, although this is not as frequent as you would think. But always wash your hands before and after handling any pet to lessen the likelihood of catching anything.

FIRST AID

First Aid kits are a must for any pet owner, whether you have a dog, cat, rabbit or a more exotic pet. You never know with animals when they are going to get themselves into a pickle and need instant urgent treatment, at least until you can get them to a vet. Your vet can advise you on what to have in your kit, but generally you should have swabs and bandages to stem any bleeding, you should also keep a note of emergency contact numbers and opening times for your regular vet, and the emergency vet.

Always try to remain calm. You are really no good at all to your rabbit if you cannot think and act in a calm rational way. If you think your rabbit has been injured, you should try and perform a brief examination yourself. It would be a good idea to ask your vet to show you to how to do this when you first take ownership of your rabbit, rather than wait until they get injured. – forewarned and forearmed is always a good policy. If you can see immediately that your rabbit is seriously injured, forget the physical examination and take your rabbit to your vet or emergency vet immediately

Below are some of the situations and injures you may encounter:

- Shock – this can be a life-threatening situation. After any traumatic injury, loss of blood even from an infection or from a medication (anaphylactic shock) your rabbit can go into shock.

- If your rabbit is in shock the symptoms to look out for are pale gums, they feel cold on their feet and/or ears, their eyes appear glassy or are closed, they may have a weak pulse, or increased rate of breathing and increased heart rate. If you feel that your rabbit may be in shock, wrap it in a towel, provide additional heat (if possible) and place the rabbit in a carrier for immediate transport to your vet;

- Bite wounds – if possible immediately flush with warm water, but if you think your rabbit maybe in shock, do not flush, but get your rabbit to the vet immediately, as attempting to clean a wound could cause more stress for your rabbit; Insect stings – can cause localised swelling;

- Back injuries – this can happen if the rabbit is not picked up correctly; Eating poisonous plants – see section listing the poison plants;

- Heat exhaustion – rabbits can only lose excessive heat through their lips, they don't pant very effectively, but they do increase the blood vessel size in their ears in an attempt to lose heat. If you suspect heat exhaustion contact your vet immediately;

- Cold – rabbits deal with low temperatures much better than they do with high temperatures, so long as they are acclimatised to the cold. Moving an indoor rabbit straight outside into cold temperatures can cause hypothermia in extreme cases.

REPRODUCTION

It is worth remembering that your doe (female rabbit) could become pregnant from the age of 4months, so be careful if she shares her hutch with an un-neutered buck (male rabbit). She may seem like she is still a baby to you, but she is now sexually mature and if you don't want the patter of around 16 tiny feet, then you need to start planning.

The pregnancy can be detected 12-14 days after mating, but if you think she may be pregnant you should contact your vet so they can check for you. After a 4-week gestation (any longer than 36 days take your rabbit to your vet), most rabbits produce a litter of 3-4 babies (kits).

You should increase her nutrition during her pregnancy, and start gradually introducing more carrots, celery, cucumber, lettuce, also increase her intake of rabbit pellets at this time.

You can provide your doe with a nesting box and this should be introduced approximately 7 days before she is due to give birth. This will keep her kits safe after they arrive as they are born deaf and blind and can't regulate their own temperatures until they are 7 days old.

2-3 days before she gives birth she will start nesting, usual signs of this are her pulling out her fur and getting an area ready for the birth. Also, at this time you should start cutting back on her food, but always ensure she has a good supply of water.

Rabbits generally give birth in the morning, and are generally trouble free. If you have concerns , remember your vet is just a phone call away. After the birth ensure the area is kept quite and calm. Any loud noises, unusual lights etc., could make her nervous and cause her to harm or even eat her babies.

Neutering (also known as 'altering')

Rabbits are very social animals, and should be kept as a pair. The ideal combination is a spayed female (doe) and a castrated male (buck).

Males

Males should be castrated if they are to be kept with entire females (although see below), or are being kept with other males and there is fighting. Un-castrated males may show sexual, territorial or dominant behaviour towards other rabbits or humans. Un-castrated males are also have a higher risk of testicular cancer.

Females

We strongly recommend neutering female rabbits. Malignant womb cancer (called Uterine Adenocarcinoma) is common in female rabbits over 5 years old. Entire females often become quite territorial and even aggressive once they reach sexual maturity (usually at 4-6 months) - they can bite, scratch and kick! They can also experience false pregnancies, during which their behaviour could become worse.

Neutered rabbits live healthier, longer lives due to the reduced risk of reproductive cancers and sexual aggression. They make better companions; as they are calmer and more loving.

When should my rabbit be neutered?

We recommend neutering male and female rabbits from 4-5 months old.

What does neutering involve?

Castration involves removal of the testicles through an incision on the scrotum.

Spaying involves the removal of the ovaries and uterus, through an incision on the rabbit's abdomen.

AILMENTS

Dacrocystitis Dacryocystitis

Dacryocystitis is a common condition in rabbits, where the tear ducts become infected and inflamed. The duct becomes obstructed, tear flowstops and prevents natural flushing from the duct causing accumulationof debris and complete blockage.

What causes it?

The nasolacrimal duct in rabbits is very bendy and runs very close tothe roots of their cheek teeth (molars). It is often related to dentaldisease due to root overgrowth or infection.

What are the signs?

White pus-like discharge at the corner of the eye, crusty or matted fur, hair loss (causing local irritation), pain/swelling around the eye, skin scalding (the area around the eye can become red and ulcerated), tear staining (on the fur around the face), can be both eyes or just one

What is the treatment?

The mainstay of treatment for this condition is to unblock the obstruction by flushing the tear ducts. There are small openings to the tear duct in the corner of each eye. We can place a small tube (cannula) into this opening to allow us to flush the tear duct with sterile saline. This procedure can usually be done while the rabbit is conscious, after administering some topical local anaesthetic drops into the eye.

If the flushing is initially unsuccessful then it may need to be repeated after treatment with some topical antibiotic eye drops. This condition can become recurrent, dependent on the cause. It is important for the vet to check the teeth properly to determine the primary cause of the blocked tear duct and dental x-rays can be of benefit here to assess the length of the tooth roots. Sedation or anaesthesia will be required to evaluate the cheek teeth and their roots fully.

Can I prevent this from happening?

Feeding a good quality, high fibre diet will help prevent dental disease. See the 'Rabbit Nutrition' handout for more information.

Dental Disease

Rabbits teeth grow continuously throughout their life; this applies to both their there incisors (front teeth) and molars (back teeth). In fact, their incisors can grow at a rate of approximately 2mm a week! The normal length is maintained by the wearing action of the upper and lower teeth working against each other. Sometimes, these teeth can overgrow; the front teeth become very long and curl or stick out at angles, and the sharp spikes form on the molar teeth.

What causes the teeth to become overgrown?

Inherited: some rabbits are born with a congenital malocclusion (present birth) - rabbits with this condition should not be bred from. Diet: lack of a good quality, high fibre diet prevents the teeth from wearing down appropriately. Trauma: young rabbits can damage their incisor teeth pulling or gnawing on the wire on their cage.

What problems can overgrown teeth cause?

Pain: dental disease can cause immense pain as the incisor teeth can grow up or down into the opposing lips, molar teeth rub on the inside of the mouth causing ulcers on the cheeks or tongue.

Runny eyes: this is a common sign of dental problems, as the overgrowth of the upper molar roots can impinge on the rabbit's tear duct, causing an overflow of tears on to the rabbit's face, which makes the area around their eye very sore and matted.

Abscesses: the roots can grow up into the eye or down into the lower jaw

Common symptoms include; weight loss, salivation, going off certain foods, runny eyes, lumps under the chin, grinding teeth, or loss of interest in their surroundings.

How is this condition treated?

Overgrown incisors can be temporarily corrected by burring down the overgrown incisors with a dental burr. This can be done while the rabbit is conscious, but it may need to be repeated every 3-4 weeks. The incisor teeth can be removed to solve the problem.

To treat malocclusion of the molar teeth, regular dentals under anaesthetic are required to allow better visualisation and examination of the molars and rasp down the rough spiky edges.

It is important to realise that long term management is essential and corrective dental work may need to be repeated.

Can I prevent my rabbit's teeth from becoming overgrown?

Yes - prevention is better than cure!

Buy your rabbit from a reputable breeder, who can assure you that only rabbits with no dental disease have been used in the breeding line.

Feed an appropriate diet - one that mimics what wild rabbits eat. They should have unlimited access to good quality hay and grass, which is high in fibre and abrasive and will help to wear the teeth down. Avoid 'muesli-type' diets as they are low in fibre and rabbits selectively feed, so instead feed small quantities of a pellet mix.

Check your rabbit's teeth on a regular basis.

Encephalitozoon Cuniculi (E.Cuniculi)

E. Cuniculi is a microscopic protozoan parasite that causes disease in rabbits. It colonises in the rabbit's brain, eyes and kidneys. Rabbits are infected by ingesting or inhaling spores which are excreted in the urine or faeces of infected animals – it can live in infected areas for several weeks. E. Cuniculi can potentially be transferred to humans but appears not to affect healthy humans. Severely immunocompromised people should avoid animals confirmed or suspected with carrying the parasite.

What are the clinical signs?

Clinical signs can be non-specific, but some of the following signs may be noted:

Nervous signs

Head tilt/neck twisting Paralysis

Weakness of the hind legs

Eventually leading to tremors/fits and then a coma

Eye disease

Cataracts and blindness

Kidney disease

Increased drinking and urination Urinary incontinence/scalding Kidney failure

Myocarditis (inflammation of the heart muscle) can be a cause of sudden death.

How is it diagnosed?

If your rabbit is showing clinical signs that point towards E. Cunicili then the vet may suggest doing a blood test which will show if they have been exposed to the parasite. If the result comes back negative this is generally conclusive and E. Cunicili can be ruled out; unless the sample is taken very early on in infection and the immune system is too weak to allow antibodies to be produced. A positive result isn't quite as easy to interpret.

How is it treated?

If E. Cuniculi is diagnosed or suspected then a 28 day course of Fenbendazole is recommended. This is available in a paste form which is given by mouth, on a daily basis. Anti-inflammatory drugs can also be given. Supportive therapy is sometimes needed depending on the severity of clinical signs, as some rabbits with severe head tilt are unable to move around or feed themselves adequately. In some cases the treatment does not improve clinical signs – usually if it is going to work, and improvement will be seen in the first week of treatment. For those rabbits who aren't responding then euthanasia may be the only option if the rabbit has no quality of life.

What is the prognosis?

The prognosis depends on the severity of clinical signs, the response to treatment and the frequency and severity of any flare ups. The main thing to bear in mind is your rabbit's quality of life, which you should discuss with your vet.

Can I stop my rabbit from getting E. Cuniculi?

First of all, you need to be 100% sure that your rabbit isn't already a carrier of the parasite – so speak to your vet about having a blood test for E. Cuniculi. If the result comes back as negative, then the best way of preventing your rabbit being infected is by preventing contact with other rabbits – domestic or wild. Bearing in mind the parasite is primarily passed on from infected urine, good hygiene is vital

– routine disinfectants should kill the spores. Other measures like raising food and water bowls off the ground to prevent urine contamination may be helpful.

Fly Strike

Fly Strike is a serious condition affecting rabbits that occurs in the summer months. In hot, humid conditions flies are attracted to dirty or soiled hindquarters and will lay their eggs around the base of their tail.

The eggs hatch within hours and turn into maggots, which feed on the rabbit's flesh, eating away at the skin and releasing toxins. This causes serious damage to the rabbit and if left can be fatal.

Rabbits at highest risk are those that suffer from:

dental problems: if your rabbit has overgrown teeth or sharp hooks (spurs) on their molars this will cause pain, preventing your rabbit from grooming properly diarrhoea: or caecotroph impaction

arthritis: your rabbit may suffer from arthritis as they get older, and will make it harder for them to turn around and groom themselves properly

skin wounds: as flies are attracted to wounds on the skin, where they lay their eggs

overweight: your rabbit will have difficulty cleaning themselves

It is essential to check your rabbit's back end and underneath at least twice a day to ensure they are clean and dry. Fly Strike can occur within a few hours!

Can I prevent my rabbit from getting Fly Strike?

YES! To protect your rabbit from getting Fly Strike, pop your rabbit down to your local practice and our qualified nurses can apply a prescription insecticidal repellent ("RearGuard") that is rubbed in to their hindquarters. This repels flies and their larvae and needs to be applied every 10 weeks throughout the spring and summer when flies are about.

How is Fly Strike treated?

If you find any maggots on your rabbit then it is important to take them to the vets straight away. We treat Fly Strike by carefully removing the maggots and eggs, clipping the fur and gently cleansing the damaged area. Supportive therapy and hospitalisation is often essential - including painkillers, antibiotics, and a drip. Fly Strike can progress very quickly and if the damage is very extensive then sometimes unfortunately euthanasia may be recommended.

Gut Stasis

Gut Stasis or ileus is a serious, but fairly common condition in rabbits where food stops moving through the gut.

If a rabbit stops eating or reduces its intake of food for any reason then its gastrointestinal system will slow down, or even come to a complete standstill. This can be fatal, even within just a matter of hours. As the guts stop moving, bacteria build up in the intestines, which release gas causing painful bloating. This further reduces the rabbit's appetite, so the rabbit becomes more dehydrated. The contents of the guts become compacted making it more difficult for the rabbit to pass them.

What are the causes of Gut Stasis?

There are many reasons a rabbit could reduce or stop eating and drinking, such as: Pain, Dental problems, Low fibre diet, Dehydration, Stress (predator, change in environment or diet, loss of a partner, extreme heat or cold and Lack of exercise.

What are the signs of Gut Stasis?

Small faeces	No faecal production
Reduced appetite	Lethargy
Hunched posture	Swollen or firm abdomen
Grinding teeth	

How is Gut Stasis treated?

If you notice any of the above signs in your rabbit then you should take them to your vet straight away. Treatment needs to be aggressive and started immediately. They are usually admitted for hospitalisation and fluid therapy (via a drip in their ear vein) to rehydrate them and help get their guts moving again. The vet may administer medication to help kick start the guts such as pro-kinetics, as well as pain relief to alleviate the discomfort due to gas build up in the intestines. Antibiotics are sometimes given. It is very important to encourage their appetite, so fresh hay and greens are offered, as well as syringe feeding a high fibre critical care diet to ensure they get the essential nutrients. If the rabbit is treated at an early stage (after only a few hours of not eating) then the prognosis is good. The longer the treatment is delayed then the less likely a good recovery is. Some rabbits require several days of hospitalisation and treatment to recover.

Mites

Cheyletiella sp also known as 'Walking Dandruff' is a fur mite that causes mild dermatitis in the rabbit. The mites are transmitted either by direct contact with another infested animal or from contaminated bedding or hay (as the female mite can live off the host in the environment for several days).

What are the signs?

The most common sign is skin irritation along the back and neck area – you may notice hair loss, scaling (dandruff), itchiness, redness and scabs.

How is it diagnosed?

It is usually possible to diagnose the condition from the clinical signs and identification of the mite. This can be done with the naked eye, brushing the coat and examining the scale (dandruff) on a dark surface, you should be able to see the mites moving around (hence the nickname 'walking dandruff'). They can also be viewed under a microscope.

How is it treated?

There are a range of treatments available including a course of fortnightly injections or topical spot-on preparations which kill the mites. Your rabbit should be re-examined at the end of the course of treatment to ensure that it has all cleared up. Any other rabbits in contact with the infected one should be treated, as the mite is very mobile and is easily transferred from rabbit to rabbit. It is important to use an appropriate insecticide as directed by your vet, as many preparations are toxic to rabbits.

It is important that the environment is treated properly to avoid re-infestation. All of the bedding and hay will need to be removed and destroyed and the hutch and living quarters thoroughly cleaned and disinfected.

Myxomatosis

Myxomatosis is a very serious and deadly viral disease that infects and kills thousands of rabbits in the UK. It infects both wild and pet rabbits, and is widespread among the wild rabbit population. It is a highly contagious disease and your rabbit can catch it from wild rabbits via direct contact, but also from fleas and other blood sucking parasites transmitting the virus. All breeds of rabbit are at risk, including indoor rabbits. Transmission of the disease is higher during the summer due to the increased numbers of fleas.

Clinical signs

A rabbit may have the disease for 5 – 14 days before showing any signs, and in this time is infectious to other rabbits. Common symptoms include puffy eyelids, purulent (pus-producing) conjunctivitis, fluid filled swellings (under the skin around the eyes, ears and genital region), lethargy/fever noisy and laboured breathing.

It is usually fatal within 2 - 3 weeks; unfortunately most rabbits with the acute form are put to sleep on humane grounds to prevent unwanted suffering. A milder/chronic form may be seen in partially immune rabbits, where the symptoms present as solid lumps over the ears and head. They may be single or multiple, and in some cases lumps may appear on the rest of the body. With proper nursing they can survive but the lumps masses may take over six months to disappear.

How can the disease be controlled?

Vaccination
A combined vaccination for Myxomatosis and Viral Haemorrhagic disease is now available for rabbits which can be given once a year. Vaccination can be started at any time, in rabbits over 6 weeks of age, but is best given around May – June, ahead of the peak Myxomatosis season in late summer/autumn. They will need a yearly booster to remain protected.

Parasite control
Keep wild rabbits away from pets and use a rabbit-specific flea treatment available from your vet. If you have other pets that come in to contact with your rabbit, like cats or dogs, ensure they are up to date with their preventative flea treatment too.

Viral Haemorrhagic Disease

Viral Haemorrhagic Disease (VHD) is a highly contagious viral disease that affects rabbits. All rabbits are at risk, even indoor rabbits. The virus is spread by direct contact between rabbits (both wild and pet rabbits), as well as by indirect contact via people, clothing, shoes, inanimate objects and fleas. The incubation period is up to 3 days but many rabbits die suddenly without showing any clinical signs. If clinical signs are apparent then they may display the following symptoms: lethargy/collapse anorexia, fever fits/convulsions difficulty breathing, blood stained nasal discharge and paralysis.

Unfortunately there is no cure available and it is almost always fatal once contracted as the virus attacks the major body organs, especially the liver, causing massive internal haemorrhage. Given the horrendous death experienced by affected rabbits, we strongly recommend that you vaccinate your rabbit. You can protect your rabbit against this deadly disease – vaccination is essential and successful. There is a combination vaccination available which vaccinates against VHD and Myxomatosis in one simple innoculation in the scruff of the neck. Your rabbit will need a booster once a year to remain protected.

Other precautions should be taken to prevent your rabbit contracting VHD:

maintaining good hygiene, always washing your hands before and after handling other rabbits

regular, up-to-date flea treatment for all in-contact pets in the household, with a suitable product from your veterinary practice, as these are potent enough to ensure the fleas and their eggs are killed.

NATURAL REMEDIES

Rabbits, getting back to nature!

Many rabbit owners are not aware that natural care and holistic health treatments are available for their pets and can also be extremely effective in a variety of conditions. Many people also do not realise that complementary medicine can offer hope when conventional treatment has failed or is unable to offer any hope of a cure.

The use of complementary medicines in rabbits has increased in recent years mainly due to: the popularity of complementary medicines for treating people and their cats, dogs and horses; there are very few conventional drugs that are licensed for use in rabbits due to the comparatively small UK rabbit population.

The very high cost of licensing a drug makes the process cost prohibitive and un-worthwhile; because rabbits do not seem to respond as well to conventional drug therapy as other animals do. For example, antibiotics are not so effective at clearing up bacterial infections. Rabbits also have what you might call a low tolerance to anaesthetics making them high-risk candidates for such procedures.

In our practice, we often use conventional medicine together with complementary medicine. However, we could not be without conventional medicine in certain situations. For example, a rabbit has been in an accident and has a broken leg. This would require a general anaesthetic, surgery and pain medication. But, as no one form of medicine can have all the answers, we feel that the best approach to medicine is the integrative approach. This is where we use both complementary and conventional medicines side-by-side to ensure the best possible healthcare is available for your rabbit.

In the above example, once the fracture has been repaired, the rabbit would be given some homoeopathic remedies such as Arnica to aid wound healing and Symphytum to aid bone healing, acupuncture may also be given to help get your bunny back on its feet as soon as possible. We may also give the Rabbit Rescue Remedy – a flower remedy to help it cope with the stress of its ordeal.

For another example of how we would help a patient with complementary medicine, imagine this scenario - a rabbit has an infected abscess. If possible we would surgically remove the abscess and then give the rabbit a herb like Echinacea to help boost its immune system, we would also apply a Calendula cream to the wound to help it heal and we may also give some flower remedies.

There are so many more healing possibilities available to us when using integrative medicine, these very different types of medicine work so well together and the wonderful thing when using integrative medicine is that the natural aspect of it, i.e. the complementary medicines, offer a tailor-made and personalised treatment course specifically for your pet.

Acupuncture – Balancing the body's energies

Acupuncture has been used on people for thousands of years in China. It is now being successfully used on pets to treat a wide range of conditions. Substantial amounts of research have confirmed that acupuncture works, and now acupuncture is accepted as a conventional treatment for animals in the USA.

The Chinese say that illness is a state of imbalance or blockage in the normal energy flows of the body and that acupuncture, acting on the channels of energy flow, restores them to normal.

Acupuncture involves the insertion of very fine needles (or the use of an acupuncture laser) into specific points of the body to produce a physiologic response, which results in a healing effect.

Acupuncture is useful in treating back pain and paralysis, chronic diarrhoea, injuries involving ligaments, tendons and muscles, sinusitis, respiratory infections and eye infections. We have also used acupuncture to help boost rabbits' immune systems.

Using the needles or laser would usually involve weekly treatments lasting about four weeks in total. In some cases, under a light anaesthetic, we insert gold beads at the acupuncture points to produce a more permanent treatment. When performed correctly acupuncture can be a very safe and effective alternative treatment.

Aromatherapy – A concentration of nature's healing powers

Aromatherapy means 'treatment using aromas'. It refers to a specific branch of herbal medicine that uses concentrated plant oils called essential oils to improve physical and emotional health, and restore balance to the whole body. (Unlike herbal medicine, essential oils are not taken internally, but are inhaled or applied to the skin.)

Essential oils are natural volatile oils with identifiable chemical and medicinal properties. Over 150 essential oils have been extracted, each one having its own scent and unique healing properties. For optimum benefits, essential oils must be extracted from natural raw ingredients and remain as pure as possible.

Whether essential oils are applied to the skin or inhaled into the lungs they are absorbed into the blood stream and are carried to every part of the body. Within the body, the essential oils are able to operate in three ways: Pharmacologically, Physiologically and Psychologically

From a pharmacological perspective, the chemical components of the oils react with the body chemistry in a way that is similar to drugs, but slower, more sympathetically and with less chance of side effects.

The oils also have physiological effects. The psychological response is triggered by the effect that the oil has on the brain. For example, Grapefruit essential oil is said to be an anti-depressant, camomile and peppermint aid digestion. Although aromatherapy has been used for centuries treating human ailments we are only recently starting to use it for rabbits. We have found it to be very useful when inhaled with steam to treat respiratory infections. As an immune booster, we use

it topically to treat skin problems like ringworm and all types of wounds on the skin. Rabbits, like people, are all individuals, and we suggest if you are going to use essential oils then you must first test your rabbit's response.

You must let the rabbit smell the chosen essential oil, because if the rabbit doesn't like the oil you won't get very far with the treatment. If the rabbit likes the essential oil then you can go ahead and use it in the correct way.

Herbal medicine – Nature's drugs

Herbal medicine is probably the oldest system of natural medicine used by people. Nothing could be more natural than harnessing the healing powers of the herbs around us to cure our diseases and those of our pets. Rabbits in the wild have a natural instinct to seek out and eat plants that will help them when they are ill and injured. Unfortunately, most pet rabbits do not have access to the plants they would naturally feed on in the wild. Today herbal medicine is still used by over 80% of the world's population. Many modern drugs are actually isolated extracts of herbs or, more commonly, synthetic derivatives of these substances. For example, aspirin is obtained from the bark of the willow tree and digitalis is obtained from the foxglove plant. Isolated extracts and synthetic compounds are more likely to cause side effects and have less overall healing power than the herbs themselves.

Although herbal medicines take longer to work, they are safer and gentler on the body than conventional drugs. They can be effectively to treat your rabbit.

In rabbits, we have successfully used herbal medicines to treat a full range of conditions that can be treated with conventional drugs. We sometimes find herbal medicines more effective than antibiotics as they help to boost the rabbit's own immune system and they do not kill off the helpful bacteria that rabbits have in their intestines.

Homoeopathy – Helping the body heal itself

Homoeopathy is a well-recognised and highly regarded system of natural that is used worldwide. Homoeopathy is safe and works in such a gentle way it produces no side effects. It views the patient as a whole and treats the individual rather than the disease. It works on the theory that homoeopathy can stimulate the body's natural defences by administering minute doses of a substance, which in larger doses may case the symptoms of an illness.

Homoeopathic remedies come from many sources – animal, vegetable and mineral. They are prepared in special ways, which involves making a solution from the original substance. This is then diluted many times with vigorous shaking at each stage to release the energy contained within the material used
Homoeopathy is based on the principles of treating like with like. When we are ill, it is as if the body has fallen out of balance.

The symptoms that the illness produces, such as an increased temperature or a bruise are indications that the body is using all its strength and vitality to fight the illness and get itself back to a normal healthy state. When we take a homoeopathic medicine to help in treating an illness we are taking a substance that can produce symptoms similar to the illness i.e. it mimics the effects of the illness, and by doing so it adds to the fighting ability of the body to combat the illness. Homoeopathy can be used to treat a surprising number of conditions that we see in our rabbit patients. It is a very safe means of treatment and is also inexpensive. We use homoeopathy frequently and like to combine it with our other forms of medicine.

Flower remedies - Emotional healers

Flower remedies were developed by Dr Edward Bach, a 1930s Harley Street Doctor. Disillusioned with some of the side effects of conventional medicine at that time, he went in search of a safer and more natural system of medicine. He was working on the theory that flowers have an enormous influence on the mind and can therefore affect our physical being too. He felt that physical illness and mental states were closely linked and that by stabilising and balancing mental or emotional problems, physical disease could be cured as a follow-on process.

Dr Bach developed a process of energising the healing potential of the energy within the flowers. He found that the action of sunlight on the petals of chosen plants that were floated on water would transfer the healing energy from the plant into the water. Dr Bach created 38 flower remedies each of which has a specific effect on mental, emotional or behavioural problems. If a physical illness seems to be linked with mental or emotional problems, the therapy will often relieve the symptoms of the physical disease as well.

We use flower remedies in our rabbit patients to treat emotional problems, we also use them as an aid to help our patients recover after chronic illnesses and also after surgery. From a behavioural point of view we use flower remedies to treat such things as aggressive bunnies, nervous and timid bunnies.

Nutraceutical – Nutritional aids

Nutraceuticals are nutritional supplements used in the treatment of disease. This is one of the fastest growth areas in human medicine. The most commonly used nutraceuticals used for rabbits are colloidal silver, pre & probiotics, vitamin and mineral supplements. Nutraceuticals offer another natural tool in the kit to help take care of your rabbit in the most natural and safe way.

I am extremely excited about the increasing use of natural medicines to treat rabbits and the concept of integrative medicine. As vets, we have a responsibility to make sure that our patients receive the very best in healthcare, using every possible medium available.

This is what we are aiming for and hopefully providing our rabbit patients with. I know that there is quite a bit of stigma attached to some of the natural therapies, please do not disregard these remedies.

They may be able to offer you another avenue of hope if your chosen one fails. I hope this article has given you some insight into what is available for your rabbit and that it may initiate further research, or even inspire you to go and seek out some integrative treatments. Whatever you take away with you from this article, I hope it will be of benefit to you and your rabbit friends.

POISONOUS PLANTS

Below are some of the more common plants that are poisonous to rabbits. This lists quite a few but is by no means the complete list.

Breed	Size Large >10lb	Size Medium 6-10lb	Size Small 2-6lb	Colours	Fur Short	Fur Long	Ear type Lop	Ear type Medium	Ear type Short	Temperament Calm	Temperament Excitable
American		✓		Blue/white	✓			✓		✓	
Angora		✓		6 colours		✓		✓		✓	
Chinchilla		✓			✓			✓		✓	
Dutch			✓	6 colours	✓			✓		✓	
Dwarf Hotot			✓	White dark eyes	✓				✓		✓
English Spot		✓		7 colours dark spots	✓			✓		✓	
Flemish Giant	✓				✓			✓		✓	✓
Harlequin		✓		4 colours	✓			✓		✓	
Rex		✓		Multi	✓			✓		✓	
Himalayan Rex			✓	White w/ black tips	✓			✓		✓	✓
Mini Rex			✓	Multi	✓			✓			✓
Satin		✓		Multi	✓			✓		✓	
Mini Satin			✓	Red, white	✓			✓			✓
Polish			✓	5 colours	✓			✓			✓
Lop		✓		many	✓		✓			✓	
Tan			✓	Black tan	✓			✓		✓	

TOP TEN TIPS FOR A HEALTHY, HAPPY RABBIT

1. Good Nutrition

2. Plenty of Water

3. Clean hutch/cage

4. Exercise

5. Company

6. Regular health checks

7. Regular grooming

8. Deworming every 3 months

9. Flea treatment once a month

10. Lots of affection

FREQUENTLY ASKED QUESTIONS

Q. What do you mean it's a girl? The breeder told me it was a boy.
A. If you are in any doubt as to the sex of your rabbit, best to check with your vet to avoid any unwanted babies.

Q. She can't be pregnant, she shares a hutch with her brother…
A. Rabbits do not care whether they are related to their hutch mate so, if unneutered they will mate.

Q. At what age can my rabbit get pregnant, and how long will she be pregnant for?
A. Medium to large size rabbits are sexually mature at around 4-5 months, while giant breeds are ready at 6-9 months. Pregnancies generally last between 31-33 days.

Q. When the babies arrive should we keep them and the mother separate from the father?
A. Yes, definitely keep them separate as the father can become aggressive, even if he doesn't normally show any temper.

Q. Is there a course of vaccination and how long before we should start?
A. There is currently one injection that covers both Myxomatosis and VHD, and that can be given from as early as 5 weeks old and would need to be repeated annually.

Q. Do you think we should allow our rabbits to have a litter before we have them neutered?
A. No, it does not cause the female rabbit any stress or long term heartache if she is neutered before she has had a litter. If you don't want babies the long term health benefits should override anything else.

Q. Why should I neuter my rabbit?
A. If you don't plan to breed from your rabbit, you should consider neutering. Neutering will calm your rabbit and will avoid unwanted pregnancy, reduce the risk of uterine cancer and lower rates of aggression - if you have same sex rabbits living together they could fight if not neuteured.

Q. Do we need to worm our rabbits like you would for dogs and cats?
A. Yes, it is important to regularly worm your rabbit to avoid an infestation of intestinal worms, and the health problems they bring.

Q. Can rabbits swim?
A. Yes, most species of wild rabbit can, the Swamp Rabbit for example, from south eastern US uses water to move about and to escape predators, usually with just his nose exposed when hiding.

Q. How many teeth does my rabbit have?
A. Rabbits actually have 28 teeth, 6 incisors, 12 upper cheek teeth and 10 lower cheek teeth.

FREQUENTLY ASKED QUESTIONS

Rabbit Welfare Association

http://www.rabbitwelfare.co.uk/pdfs/Hutch

RSPCA

http://www.rspca.org.uk

House Rabbit Society

http://www.myhouserabbit.com

Printed in Great Britain
by Amazon